HIGHLIGHT jamaica

Written and photographed by

DAVE SAUNDERS

The publisher –
To Chris Humphrys, thanks for the idea, patience and understanding.

The author –
To Fran, Fil and Vikki who shared the experience.

MOWGLI BOOKS

in association with

The Novelty Trading Co. Ltd.

INTRODUCTION

LIKE the planters' punch, Jamaica can hit you right between the eyes. The mountains are breath-taking, the beaches idyllic and the vegetation luxuriant. The warm, tropical climate has made sure of that. So it's hardly surprising that many visitors return to Jamaica again and again.

"'Tis the fairest isle eyes have seen," wrote Christopher Columbus in 1494, when he came across this effervescent little island set like a jewel in the Caribbean Sea.

Columbus was responsible for the misnomer 'West Indies'. About 500 years ago when he arrived here he thought he had reached the East Indies. The name 'Caribbean' comes from the fierce Carib Indians who lived on several of the islands before Europeans arrived.

At that time, Jamaica was inhabited by peaceful Arawak Indians, who lived by fishing and farming. The island's name comes from the Arawak word 'Xaymaca', meaning 'Land of wood and water'.

Jamaica is approximately 150 miles long and 50 miles wide – about the size of Connecticut or Northern

Ireland. It's the third largest Caribbean island, the largest English-speaking island in the Caribbean and home for over two and a half million.

Your first experience of Jamaica comes as you step out of the muted sophistication of the plane straight into the open-air sauna of Kingston or Montego Bay airport. The humidity enfolds you like a warm, moist blanket. This is no time to rush around getting hot and bothered. It's time to slow down to a Caribbean pace of life. Take it easy. Soon come. No problem.

Jamaica is a rich and colourful tapestry. A feast for the senses. A Caribbean cocktail of sights, sounds and smells. It's much more than a beach, it's a country. So join us and discover Jamaica...

Above: *Heliconia or Lobster claw is a member of the banana family.*

Below: *White River east of Ocho Rios.*

Right: *Rastaman in Montego Bay craft market.*

MANGO

OVERVIEW

Above left:
Today Newcastle is used as a base for training soldiers of the Jamaica Defence Force.

Above:
A country road with Cockpit Country in the background.

THE Jamaican flag was first hoisted in Kingston's National Stadium on 6th August 1962 when Jamaica gained its independence from Britain. Alexander Bustamante was appointed the first Prime Minister.

The gold diagonal lines represent sunlight and the natural wealth of the country. Triangles of black signify hardships that the country has overcome and the difficulties still to be faced. The green triangles represent hope and agricultural wealth.

Unlike many pancake-like islands of the Caribbean, Jamaica is dominated by a mountainous backbone of rugged highland, rising to the 7,402 ft, Blue Mountain Peak north of Kingston. In an area to the west known as Cockpit Country, the pitted woodland resembles the inside of a huge green eggbox. It was to these inaccessible hills that the slaves of the Spanish escaped over 300 years ago.

Some 4,000 ft up in the Blue Mountains sits Newcastle. Built by the British army in 1841, it was used as a retreat and rehabilitation centre for soldiers and officers suffering from yellow fever or malaria. At one time it was known as the sanatorium of Kingston.

Bauxite, Jamaica's 'red gold' is extracted by open-cast mining, then converted into alumina and aluminium. The red soil is taken by rail to one of a number of coastal ports, such as at Discovery Bay and Ocho Rios. From here it is shipped to alumina factories in the USA and Canada.

Jamaica is clothed in colourful blooms. Lignum vitae, hibiscus, frangipani, allamanda, orange trumpet vine... nearly 3,000 varieties of flowering plants grow here, thanks to Jamaica's tropical climate.

Above left: *Bauxite deposits near the surface are extracted by open – cast mining.*

Below left: *Kaiser Bauxite's Port Rhodes pier at Discovery Bay.*

Above right: *Hibiscus flowers come in many shapes, sizes, colours and bloom throughout the year.*

Right: *The red ginger plant has waxy red bracts and small whitish blooms.*

Below: *Frangipani's pink, yellow or white blossoms have a strong, sweet fragrance.*

Trade winds bring rain to the north-east of the island. Yet to the south, in the rain shadow, the air is dry and there are few trees to give shade. Here you will find the silver thatch palm, one of the few trees which can survive in this dry region. Its leaves are used to make hats and baskets as well as providing roofing material for some houses. Here, too, are several varieties of cacti. The most common are the upright columns which grow in spiky forests alongside prickly pear and climbing cacti.

For many years Ian Fleming lived in Jamaica, and during that time he wrote one book each year. He named his hero after James Bond, author of the book *Birds of the West Indies*.

Jamaica has over 250 species of birds. One of these, the Doctor Bird, is found in no other country in the world. It is the country's national bird, and a stylized drawing of the Doctor Bird is used in the Air Jamaica logo.

Below and right: *Found only in Jamaica, the Doctor Bird, or streamer tail hummingbird, is one of many species that gather each afternoon to be fed on Lisa Salmon's verandah near Anchovy south of Montego Bay.*

Sugar cane, once the mainstay of the Jamaican economy, is still the leading export crop. Large estates control about half of the cane growing, while small farmers supply the rest. The cane is harvested between January and July. The evening before it is cut, the field is burned to kill off insects and destroy the dead leaves or 'trash'. As the cane burns it gives off a distinctive aroma of burnt sugar and the leaping flames can be seen for miles around.

Much of the cane is harvested by hand using a long knife or machete. It is dirty, back-breaking work, yet Jamaican cutters are considered among the most proficient in the world. Many go to the southern states of the USA to harvest cane.

Originally donkeys were used to help crush the cane to extract the sweet juices. Besides producing sugar for export, molasses from cane is used as stock feed or distilled to make alcohol, and bagasse (dry cane fibre) goes to make chipboard or is used for fuel. Sugar is the raw material for rum, and Jamaican rum is famous throughout the world.

***Above:** The original method of crushing sugar cane is demonstrated at the Appleton Estate.*

***Right:** Byron Henry presents a strong rum punch as a finale to a tour of the Appleton factory.*

Although the people of Jamaica originate from Africa, China, India and Europe, they have evolved a national pride and sense of identity which unites them. The country's motto is 'Out of many, one people'. You will see a great range of skin colours from white to black-black, often with very handsome features.

Jamican patios evolved during the time of slavery 300 years ago. Workers from different tribes used some of the words and grammar of their British masters, combined with their own African languages.

KINGSTON

PEOPLE are drawn to Jamaica's capital for both business and pleasure. It is the centre for the island's culture, craft and history. Kingston's waterfront skyline is dominated by concrete and glass hotels and office blocks. Here, the Jamaica Conference Center was opened by the Queen of England in February 1983. The building has blended United Nations specifications with a uniquely Jamaican identity. Walls and ceilings are adorned with bamboo, wicker, coral, shells and tropical vegetation.

Left: *The Jamican Conference Center.*

Insert: *Kingston waterfront.*

Below: *The Bank of Jamaica on Kingston's waterfront.*

Acquired by the Jamaican National Trust in 1967, Devon House *(preceding pages)* has been restored as a showroom for Jamaican crafts.

Vale Royal, the official residence of the Prime Minister of Jamaica, is one of the oldest continuously owned homes on the island, believed to have been built around 1694.

The statue of Norman Manley, who co-founded the People's National Party in 1938, stands at the entrance of Parade Park.

I THREE

Reggae first hit the streets of West Kingston in the early 1960s. Spearheaded by Bob Marley and the Wailers, it became the international voice of the oppressed.

Bob Marley's statue stands outside the Marley Museum on Hope Road.

Disused stone aquaducts once supplied water to the Mona and Papine sugar estates, and now decorate the campus of the University of the West Indies, as does a large mural *(above)* depicting aspects of Jamaican life.

Built for the Central American and Caribbean Games in 1962, the National Stadium is Jamaica's major sports venue. In front of the stadium is the powerful statue of 'The Jamaican Athlete' *(preceding pages)*.

Once a race track, National Heroes Park was laid out as the final resting place of Jamaica's National Heroes, including:
Alexander Bustamante *(left)*
Norman Manley *(centre)*
and Marcus Garvey *(right)*.

Across the harbour is Port Royal, at the tip of the Palisadoes peninsula. Within a year of arriving in Jamaica in 1655, the English started building a fort here to guard the entrance to the harbour. It soon became a wealthy and wicked base for swashbuckling buccaneers led by Henry Morgan. But divine retribution had the final word in 1692 when an earthquake and tidal wave drowned two thirds of the town.

Hurricane Gilbert struck Jamaica in September 1988. The hurricane was one of the most ferocious the island has ever experienced. On the road to Norman Manley Airport stands a monument to its destructive force *(following pages).*

Left: *The rejuvenated face of Fort Charles at Port Royal.*

Below: *The hurricane tears through the name 'Gilbert' painted on an old oil drum.*

PRIVATE
PP 1969

NO PARKING
NO WAITING

There are nearly as many religious demoninations as there are churches in Jamaica. Most people feel close to their religion and many sects meet for worship several times a week. Kumina is a religious cult which originated in the Congo (now Zaire) in Africa. The ceremonies are centered around heavy drumming, dancing and possession by ancestral spirits. Miss Queenie is the Kumina queen or priestess. As the drumming and singing become more insistent, Queenie works herself into a trance. She believes she becomes possessed by spirits of her ancestors.

Above: *Anglican Parish Church of St. John in Black River.*
Right: *The Cathedral of St. Jago de la Vega in Spanish Town.*

Around the central square in Spanish Town, just 14 miles west of Kingston, stands the sculpted Italian marble of the Rodney Memorial and the colonnaded building of the parish council offices of St. Catherine.

The Spanish abandoned their first settlement at Seville in 1534 and established their capital in Spanish Town, calling it Villa de la Vega, town on the plain. It was later called St. Jago de la Vega after St. James of Compostella the patron saint of Spain. This was the Spanish capital of Jamaica for more than 100 years, and the British capital for two years.

PN

HERO

MANDEVILLE

ON market day buses and trucks from villages outside the main towns load up with produce from the fields. Then, heaving with pumpkin, peppers and people, they career round the narrow roads, horns blaring.

Some of Mandeville market is housed in a proper building, but makeshift stalls spill out into Park Crescent. Goods are spread out on wooden tables, in cardboard boxes or on rough mats. Green bananas are stacked by the wall still on their stems. Bukets full of fish in brine slosh about as someone knocks passed them.

A woman with a knitted woollen hat sits on an upturned crate and calls out "Come buy me mango... Yu wan pineapple, pear, ackee?"

When ripe, the ackee bursts open, revealing a fleshy substance that tastes something like buttery scrambled egg, and is usually eaten with 'sal'fish' (salted cod.)

Below: *Ackee tree.*

Below right: *Jelly coconuts provide a refreshing drink.*

PORT ANTONIO

PORT Antonio is the old banana capital of Jamaica. There are over 300 edible types of banana. Some taste like strawberries, others like apples. Plantain is a large banana which is baked or fried before eating. Green bananas are cooked as a vegetable. The purple banana 'flower' (*below*) peels back to reveal a 'hand' of small green bananas which then grow and ripen.

Port Antonio is also a place where writers and artists come for inspiration and solitude. Robin Moore wrote *The French Connection* here under a mango tree in his garden. Errol Flynn owned the nearby Navy Island.

Noel Coward's house 'Firefly' commands a superb view of Port Maria a few miles along the coast.

Errol Flynn popularized rafting down the Rio Grande, drifting serenely on a bamboo raft through cassia, banana and bamboo.

Several exclusive hotels are situated along the coast. Some are clifftop retreats, such as Trident Hotel *(main picture)*. Others dip their silvery, palm-fringed beaches into the opalescent water.

Legend has it that the Folly *(below)*, to the east of Port Antonio, was built by a rich man for his bride. In his haste to complete it he used sea water to mix the concrete. As a result the edifice began to crumble as he carried her across the threshold. The true story is less romantic: it was built by a jeweller from Connecticut in 1905. Far from being a young bride, his wife was already a grandmother when they moved in! Since then, others have followed similar grandiose dreams and built striking symbols of their success, such as Earl Levy's castle (*above*).

Keep a sharp lookout as you travel along the north coast, you may catch sight of a small wooden shack advertising 'Jerk Pork' or 'Jerk Chicken'. The meat is well-seasoned and pepper-hot, with numerous spices.

Blue Mountain coffee is famous throughout the world. Coffee bushes grow best on hill slopes between 3,000 ft and 5,000 ft. As it is cooler at this altitude, the berries takes longer to ripen and this gives them more flavour. Coffee berries are red when ripe. The crop is harvested between September and February, then the skins are removed and the beans are dried.

OCHO RIOS

OCHO Rios is Jamaica's fastest-growing north coast resort. From Shaw Park Gardens you can look out over the crescent-shaped bay with its fringing white sand.

Cruise ships call frequently to give passengers a brief glimpse of the island. Large luxury liners berth at the wharf near the Reynolds bauxite terminal at Deep Water pier. Passengers are often greeted by an old mento or calypso band. While the cruise ships are in, the town comes to life, and the price of crafts, food and taxis soars.

Ocho Rios does not mean 'eight rivers', but comes from the Spanish *Las Chorreras*, meaning 'the waterfalls'.

It is not difficult to see why Jamaica is called "the land of wood and water". The island's most famous waterfall is Dunn's River Falls near Ocho Rios *(preceding pages)*. The natural 600 ft limestone staircase is constantly washed by swirling, pummelling water. A nearby waterfall provides a stunning backdrop to 'The Ruins' restaurant in Ocho Rios *(below)*. Two of Jamaica's lesser known waterfalls are Reach Falls, near Manchioneal at the eastern end of the island, and YS Falls in the south west *(right and far right)*.

Above: *Cricket at St. Mary Sports Club is overlooked by Gray's Inn Great House.*

Left: *South of Ocho Rios, Fern Gully follows a former river bed.*

Below: *Dominoes is a national pastime played with vigour and vitality.*

Right: *A statue of Christopher Columbus stands near St. Ann's Bay.*

MONTEGO BAY

Above: *View over Montego Bay from Richmond Hill Inn.*

Far left: *Sam Sharpe Square was named after the rebel slave leader who was made a National Hero.*

Left: *Doctor's Cave Beach.*

MONTEGO Bay, known affectionately as 'Mobay', is Jamaica's second city and the traditional tourist capital of the island.

Jamaica's most famous beach, Doctor's Cave, took its name from a small nearby cave that no longer exists, and its one-time owner, Dr. Alexander McCatty.

During the time of slavery, when the large sugar and banana plantations were established, the master of the estate lived in a big house called a Great House. Some of them are maintained as private houses, but many have been converted into hotels or public buildings.

About 10 miles east of Mobay, Rose Hall is the most infamous Great House in Jamaica, thanks to the strange tales of Annie Palmer, the White Witch. It is said that Annie Palmer used to seduce men (slaves and husbands alike) and then murder them in macabre ways. In 1831 she was herself murdered by some of the slaves, and her ghost, or *duppy*, is said to ride on horseback through the night.

Street traders or hawkers are called higglers. You can haggle with the higglers for sack-cloth trousers, 'Jamaica, no problem' T-shirts, strings of colourful bead necklaces or black coral bracelets.

Rastafarianism has provided a rich well of inspiration for clothes, carvings and music. Red, yellow and green Rasta colours adorn belts and tams, boats and buildings. The head and dreadlocks of the Rastaman provide a striking subject, especially when carved into a tree trunk.

Rastas take the Bible literally when it says "no razor may be used on his head... he must let the hair of his head grow long." (Numbers 6, verse 5), and so they never cut their hair. In November 1930 Ras (Prince) Tafari was crowned Emperor Haile Selassie 1 of Ethiopia. Many of the oppressed took the new king's name as their banner, and became known as Rastafarians.

NEGRIL

NEGRIL, at the sunset end of the island, is the 'anything goes' capital of Jamaica. Barefoot and Bohemian. Somewhere to give your body a holiday while putting your mind into neutral.

For centuries Negril was detached from the rest of the country by the Great Morass, swampy land which was difficult to cross. The seven miles of sandy, palm-fringed beach dipping into clear water stocked with beautiful corrals was known only to local fishermen until its secret was discovered and the area was opened up.

It wasn't until 1965 that Negril's first hotel, The Sundowner, now a part of Sandals Resort, began catering for a select group of guests. Negril has never looked back since then, yet, even now, no building is higher than the tallest coconut palm.

The reefs off Negril are excellent for scuba diving and snorkeling. Other watersports include parasailing, sailing, windsurfing, water skiing and jet skiing.

Left: *At the northern end of Negril's beach is a small island called Booby Cay, which appeared in the movie 20,000 Leagues Under The Sea.*

Jamaica is surrounded by a sea full of beautiful fish. The country's fishing industry is small scale, and many fishermen operate from the beach, some with only a small canoe hollowed out from an old cotton tree. They often fish during the night and return with just a few pounds of fish, which are sold on the beach or taken to a nearby market.

Many conch are collected from around the shores and are fried in batter, used in soup or as bait. The conch is removed by making a gash in the shell, which releases the animal's hold and allows it to be pulled out. Piles of broken conch shells are strewn over all the fishing beaches around the island.

About half the country's fish requirement is imported, including the salted cod for one of Jamaica's national dishes - 'ackee and sal' fish'.

Above: *Fishermen setting out at dusk.*

Far left: *Sunset in Negril.*

Following pages: *The sun breaks through the clouds to mark the end of an afternoon thunder storm.*

As evening deepens, a dog barks in the distance, music sifts through the balmy evening air and mingles with the nightly choir of tiny whistling toads. Moths congregate around flickering lamps and fireflies blink incessantly in the dark. As you sit on your verandah watching the sun melt into the sea, you close your eyes and let the lure of Jamaica seep into your blood along with the rum, the reggae and your resolve to return.